# Now What Do I Do?
## 15 Essential Steps to Handling Various Situations

We often find ourselves in challenging situations where we have no idea how to deal with them effectively. Pre-thinking scenarios adds tools to our tool bag so that we can be more productive when faced with difficult situations.

Reading this book you will know:
- What to consider when making important decisions.
- What home remedies can handle emergencies.
- How to stay physically safe in unknown environments.
- How to handle unwanted spam.
- How you say something is more important than what you say.

**If you are intending to increase your ideas on how to creatively solve life's challenges pick up this Itty Bitty Book today.**

# Your Amazing Itty Bitty® What Happens When Book

*15 Essential Steps On How To Handle Various Situations*

Sharón Lynn Wyeth

Published by Itty Bitty® Publishing
A subsidiary of S & P Productions, Inc.

Copyright © 2020 **Sharón Lynn Wyeth**

All rights reserved. No part of this book may be reproduced or transmitted in any form or by any means, electronic or mechanical, including photocopying, recording or by any information storage and retrieval system, without written permission of the publisher, except for inclusion of brief quotations in a review.

Printed in the United States of America

Itty Bitty Publishing
311 Main Street, Suite D
El Segundo, CA 90245
(310) 640-8885

ISBN: 978-1-950326-59-4

*Dedication*

This book is dedicated to people who were never taught how to appropriately handle various challenging situations that may occur in life and to my dad, may he rest in peace, knowing how much he influenced my life and that his teachings continue to help others.

Stop by our Itty Bitty® website Directory to find out interesting information about how to handle life's situations.

www.IttyBittyPublishing.com

Or visit Sharón Lynn Wyeth at:

www.KnowTheName.com

www.TheNameLady.com

## Table of Contents

Introduction
Situation 1. Stranger on Your Doorstep
Situation 2. Refreshments at Social Events
Situation 3. Unwanted Spam
Situation 4. Bodily Endangerments
Situation 5. Choking on Food
Situation 6. Home Remedies
Situation 7. Making Important Decisions
Situation 8. Choose Your Words Wisely
Situation 9 Always Be Aware of Your Surroundings
Situation 10. Seasonal Discount Shopping
Situation 11. Rules to Live By
Situation 12. Eating Habits for Maximum Health
Situation 13. Taking Risks Involving Money
Situation 14. Compassion
Situation 15. Live by Your Own Rules

## Introduction

I was fortunate to have a father who led discussions every night at the dinner table. He would come up with different scenarios based on life situations that had occurred in the newspaper or in his doctor's office to lead us children into conversations that would teach us how to discern truth, how to look beyond the obvious, and how to consider possible consequences when problem solving. This book shares with you some of my dad's way of dealing with situations.

# Situation 1
**Stranger on Your Doorstep**

The question posed to us five kids one night at the dinner table was, "What would you do if there was a knock on the door and the person on the other side of the door stated that he was a policeman and he needed to use your phone?" Now this was before the age of mobile phones, however, the thinking process that was shared is still valuable today.

1. Would you open the door and simply let the policeman inside to use your phone?
2. Would you volunteer to make the call for him?
3. Would you simply assume that he was telling us the truth because policemen don't lie?

What would you do in this situation?

The first question to ask yourself is how do you know if he is really a policeman? If you ask for a badge number as proof remember that anyone could make up a number and you wouldn't know if it was true or not. Before opening your door to any stranger there are appropriate steps to take. Do you know what they are?

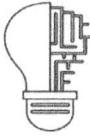

## Verification Comes First

In this case the steps are:

- Ask for the policeman's name and badge number.
- Call the precinct and ask if this policeman with this badge number should be in your area.
- Report that the person at the door is requesting to come inside to use your phone and for them to send appropriate aid to that person.
- Never open the door as you have no idea what that person's real intent is once he is in your house.

This scenario came in handy when I was a high school administrator as a policeman came into our school requesting to speak to a student. Since administrators act as substitute parents until the parent can arrive, I asked for him to be seated and I'd retrieve the student. First though, I stopped in my office and called the police precinct asking if that policeman should be at my school. In this case he should not. So, I returned to the attendance office to let the man know that the child was finishing up a test and could he kindly wait the 10-15 minutes for her to finish. That was how long it would take the real cops to get to my school. A child's life was protected because of my father's teachings.

# Situation 2
## Refreshments at Social Events

We often assume that the refreshments served are safe to eat when invited to a social function. However, my father did not make that assumption as he had seen too many people in the emergency room at the hospital because of something consumed that was thought to be safe. Thus, he asked us, how can you tell if something you are going to eat is safe for consumption?

1. Is it safe because you know the cook?
2. Is it safe because you are at a friend's house?
3. Is it safe because you are in a restaurant?
4. Is it safe because you are at a party with people you know?
5. Is it safe because a friend served it to you?
6. Is it safe because others are eating it?

Ask yourself, how do you know if something is safe to consume?

## Never Assume Refreshments Are Safe

Dad instructed us not to trust anything that was in an open container or made by someone you didn't know, or whose kitchen you had not seen.

- When holding a soda can keep your thumb over the opening when not drinking so that no one could slip something into your drink when you are not looking.
- When drinking from an open glass to hold your other hand over the large opening at the top of the glass.
- When needing to go to the restroom, either take the glass with you or to dump it out, as again, anything could be added when you are away. Also, remember this in restaurants when dining with someone you don't know well.
- Unless you know the cooks well, do not eat anything that is not prepackaged.

This training came in handy when Central Office personnel were served a delicious looking lunch made by PTA parents in appreciation of educators. All of us attended. I ate nothing as I was not familiar with the kitchens of these parents. A week after the event we were informed that one of the parents had hepatitis and that all of us needed to be tested. Once again, following my dad's directives kept me safe since I hadn't eaten. Remember this at potlucks!

# Situation 3
## Unwanted Spam

Today we are all bombarded with spam and it appears that we cannot escape the intrusions into our lives via unwanted e-mails, unwanted phone calls, and unwanted mail in our mail boxes. What actions can you take to eliminate spam?

1. Write to the spammers and request that they stop sending you unrequested items.
2. Call the spammers and state you'd like to be taken off of their list.
3. Block the spammers and hope that takes care of it.
4. Put your name on a DO NOT CALL list.

Unfortunately contacting spammers doesn't work because contacting them verifies your e-mail address and/or phone number. Now the spammers can sell your information to others and/or use it on their various other spam lists.

Blocking spammers doesn't work well as most simply continue to send mail from a different address. Adding your name to the DO NOT CALL list wastes your time as spammers continually use new phone numbers.

So, what do you do? What is your solution?

## Spam the Spammers

When nothing appears to work to stop uninvited spam follow these suggestions.

- Blocking e-mail addresses, labeling them as spam, and unsubscribing when possible is about the best you can do with unwanted e-mails, along with putting key words into your spam definitions folder whereas your provider will automatically label some e-mails as spam.
- Open unwanted mail that arrives in your mailbox and using their postage paid envelope return their spam to them. This takes their time to open the mail, and their money on the return postage. Result is that you'll quickly get taken off of their lists.
- Write down the spam phone numbers identified on your phone prior to blocking that number. Then when surfing the Internet and you are requested to put in a phone number before you can get the information you seek, use those spam numbers that you have collected.

Problems will continue until enough citizens refuse to pay to stop the ads on their mobile phones instead choosing to close their accounts if ads and spam continues; and demand that lawmakers actually do something about these problems.. However, in the meantime, have fun spamming the spammers.

# Situation 4
## Bodily Endangerment

There are different times when someone else's actions put you in a dangerous situation which is why it's important to always be aware of your surroundings and to take preemptive actions. What would you do in these situations?

1. Someone starts to follow you as you are walking down the otherwise empty street.
2. A person and his partner literally grab you where you can't move, and the weather is so bad that no one else is outside.
3. You are stuck overnight in a foreign airport.
4. You are stuck in your car in the middle of nowhere in a freezing storm and cannot see the road well enough to drive more.

It is always an excellent idea to consider various situations prior to them occurring and to figure out what you would do. What would you do in each of these situations to ensure you stay safe?

## Constantly Think Safety First

Each of these situations has happened to me. Having been instructed by dad, this is what I did in each case.

- I noticed that I was being followed and when I stopped to look around the person behind me would duck into doorways. Realizing that I was an easy target to have my purse stolen as no one else was out walking, I entered the next public building, a bank, and called Lyft.
- Most people when they start to attack you are thrown off by crazy people. I started shaking uncontrollably and repeatedly muttered the same sentence until the huge man who held me let me go stating to his partner that it was not worth dealing with a crazy person.
- Find a bathroom stall that is against two of the room's walls. Put your luggage in the corner where the walls meet and sleep in the stall unless you are capable of staying awake all night.
- Keeping all of your windows rolled up in your car in freezing weather causes your car to act like a refrigerator and you can literally freeze to death. Crack your windows open when staying in your car in frigid weather. Carry emergency supplies, including a blanket, water, first aid kit, snacks, in your trunk at all times.

# Situation 5
## Choking on Food

It is not uncommon when a person is eating for them to suddenly start choking on their food. It is dangerous for the one chocking and equally scary for the others eating nearby if they don't know how to help the person who is choking.

So, what would you do if you started chocking on your food?

1. Will you attempt to swallow as much water as possible in an attempt to push the stuck food down your throat?
2. Will you signal to others that you need help and hope others know what to do?
3. Will you grab your throat and do your best to swallow?
4. Would the hemlock maneuver work for your situation and will you hope that someone gets to you quickly enough?

How do you unstick the food that is stuck to be able to stop choking? How quickly can you assess your situation when you are the one who is choking?

## Saving Yourself When Choking

Knowing a bit of physical anatomy is important.

- The first thing to do when choking is to raise your left arm high in the air as it opens up the throat where it's easier for the body to pass the stuck object through the laryngeal pharynx passageway.
- If you don't remember which arm is to be raised, as raising the right one doesn't open the passageway, raise both arms up in the air.
- If necessary to gain another person's attention in a busy restaurant, push your plate and glass off the table so that it makes enough noise crashing to the floor so that all attention is now on you.

Many students ate their lunches in my classroom instead of the cafeteria. Occasionally a student would start to choke on their food. I'd immediately tell the student to raise their left arm, and often needed to simply change the directions to raising both arms. So many students were surprised that this simple solution worked, and that they hadn't learned this solution in their own homes. However, sometimes more is required.

Twice I've choked in restaurants and remain grateful that other diners knew how to assist me. Once, I choked when not alone. My companions didn't notice until I knocked over my water glass.

## Situation 6
### Home Remedies

When Dad would diagnose an illness for a patient he would start with the common causes for that ailment. He often said, *"Common things happen more commonly than uncommon things."* Only if the common solution didn't solve the problem would he explore other options.

Do you know the common solution to the following?

1. How to stop a bee sting from stinging?
2. When sprayed by a skunk, how do you get rid of the odor?
3. How to stop jellyfish stings from burning?
4. How to get your bearings when tumbled by ocean waves?
5. What can you eat when sick?
6. How to settle your stomach when you feel like vomiting?
7. How to clear out a stuffy nose and break up chest congestions quickly.

## Knowledge Passed Through Generations

Milk and dairy may cause inflammation when taken internally, yet externally milk is a miracle cure.
- Unknowingly I put my hand on top of five bees when bracing myself. Talk about pain from those stings. However, soaking my hand in milk reduced the swelling and vanquished the pain.
- Taking a milk bath eliminates a skunk's odors for humans and animals.

Oceans can be great fun until stung by jellyfish or tumbled under powerful currents and/or waves.
- Put wet sand on your skin where the jellyfish stung you. Keep replacing with more wet sand until the sting goes away which is surprisingly quick.
- People drown when tossed around in the ocean because they run out of breath before being able to determine which way is up. Bubbles always rise to the surface, so open your eyes, blow bubbles, and follow their direction.

Too many students got food poisoning while on a week-long school trip. I stayed with the ones who were vomiting, settling their stomachs with clear carbonated sodas, rubbing Vick's Vaper Rub on their feet's arches to break up their congestion, and providing Campbell's Chicken Soup when hungry. All were better in 24 hours.

# Situation 7
## Making Important Decisions

Making important decisions can be challenging because you want to be sure you are making the best decision possible. It's too easy to make a rash decision that is regretted later, or a stupid decision as it wasn't well thought out. So, how do you go about making those most important decisions?

1. Do you ask your friends and family to make the decision for you?
2. Do you research and gather as much information as possible?
3. Do you flip a coin?
4. Do you make a decision by default, which is not making a decision, instead choosing to wait and see what happens?
5. Do you abdicate making the decision allowing societal rules make it for you?

It's important to make your own decisions so that you cannot blame the results on someone else. Plus, you won't wonder later would things have turned out differently if you had made the decision? Yet, knowing, without any doubt, that you've made the right choice is challenging.

What process do you use to be sure you've made the best decision?

# Decision Making Methodology

Fold a paper in half lengthwise. Label the left side CONS and the right-side PROS. What are your advantages and disadvantages of taking your desired action? Put your thoughts about the decision on the appropriate side of paper.

Keep this list with you for an entire two weeks constantly adding pros and cons as they are considered. Do not judge or evaluate any item in either column until the end of the two weeks when it becomes time to value the items.

- Does one item on either side of the pros or cons jump out and negate all of the items on the other side of the paper?
- Which side is longer?

You now have all of the facts required to really consider all of your options and whether the pros or the cons ought to win.

- Are your choices legal?
- Will you learn something new with this action?
- Will this create a win-win situation if working with someone else?

All three of these statements ought to be true before proceeding. Thus, you can now make the best educated decision possible.

# Situation 8
## Choose Your Words Wisely

Once said we cannot take back any words that have been spoken. Thus, it's important to think before we speak. How we decide to say something is also important. For example: in Spanish hunger is expressed as "I have hunger" ("Tengo hombre") versus in English we say, "I am hungry." Yet, the words I AM refers to our Creator, so not to use the words I AM unless speaking of the God spark within self.

Dad also encouraged us to dissect words and to think about what words are really appropriate to say. Examples of this are:

1. We don't *use* people's services, we *utilize* them.
2. We never give *advice* to someone, as we don't *add vice* to their lives. Instead, make suggestions, and don't do so until asked by the other person.
3. *Television* is simply a machine that tells (*tele*) lies to our eyes (*vision*).
4. People cannot have intimate relationships until they know self well as *intimacy* is *in-to-me-see*.
5. *Disease* is physically being uncomfortable; *dis-ease* of the body.

# Proper Utilization of Words for the Situation

We never know when something we have said or done absolutely rubs someone the wrong way. So, if our intents were pure, then we may be at fault but we will not feel guilty or have remorse as our intentions were to assist and never to harm. This is especially important on social media. What do you do with negative comments on your account?

- Do you make a nasty comment back?
- Do you judge the person?
- Do you talk badly about the other person?
- Do you justify your statements?
- Do you make a longer comment that degrades the other person?
- Do you try to rally others to agree with your cause?

What do you say or do when you feel like you are under attack from someone else either online or in person?

Dad stated not to attack back as it causes conflict; however, do affirm yourself in front of the other person. Thus, letting them know their cruel words did not bother you and you still think the same about yourself as you did prior to their nastiness.

# Situation 9
## Always Be Aware of Your Surroundings

Dad was big on staying safe and thinking safety in any situation or place that we might find ourselves. Thus, he gave us drills on where to sit in an auditorium so that if there was a fire we'd be close to an exit, or if there was an explosion we'd be away from the exploding glass. He told us to always notice where the exits were when we entered a place and not to sit with our backs to the door so that we could monitor what was happening. This was not to create fear in us, as fear was simply a lack of information. Instead, this was to create a feeling that we were always safe wherever we were and we'd know when to leave if the situation became unsafe.

What would you do if a person with a gun entered into the area where you are?

1. Immediately rush for the exit?
2. Drop to the floor and play dead?
3. Drop to the floor and attempt to crawl out unseen?
4. Hide behind something that could stop the bullets?
5. Attempt to call for help on your phone?
6. Be too scared to do anything?

## People Utilizing Guns to Gain Control Are Always Dangerous

Dad indicated that there is no reasoning with people who are mad enough to come into any establishment and start shooting. You must know where your exits are and already have a plan. For example, if caught in a large auditorium with a lot of people you can slip out the side doors unless you're sitting in the middle of the theater. Then, your best bet would be to lay on the ground beneath the seats.

- Notice where the exits are of each building you visit.
- Make a plan the first time in that building where the safest places are to sit so you'll always know.
- Sit towards the back of the area so you'll have more time to react should someone start something when they enter the space, but only if there is a back exit.

My daughter and I were shopping for clothes for her and were in the dressing room when an angry man came into the small shop yelling and demanding everyone follow his directions. I instructed my daughter to quickly dress in her own clothes as we needed to exit the back of the store to safety. We exited without being seen and were then able to call for help for the others.

# Situation 10
## Seasonal Discount Shopping

Everything has a season. Foods grow according to their seasons and stores put certain items on sale during their specific timing. You already know this, but maybe not consciously. He said notice what goes on sale after which holidays and purchase then.

1. You know that each August school supplies go on sale. That is the time to purchase school supplies for the entire year, including your home office. Here are some of dad's seasons that he had noticed.
2. March – dismal time for sales as everyone is out for Spring Break and bored, so they don't need to attract sales.
3. Travel sales start after the kids are back in school, as do travel packages
4. Candy goes on sale in November after Halloween. Freeze it and its good for next year.
5. October – weather is changing so time to sell outdoor furniture, and appliances
6. November has the best sales of the year due to Black Friday items.
7. December – nothing

## Seasonal Timings on Situations

This idea of seasons can be applied further to help monitor your choices or behaviors.

- Police give out more tickets at the end of the month than any other time. Police may say they don't have a quota, yet if they don't write an average number of tickets, it indicates that they weren't doing their job. Hence, they will write extra ones towards the end of the month to make sure their numbers are within the normal range. So, be exact on driving the speed limits towards the end of each month.

- Summer is the time to do your holiday shopping, or immediately after the holidays. Since all merchandise goes on sale immediately after the holidays, why not give gift certificates so people can shop after the holidays and get more for the same amount that you would spend on them? Or, shop during the summer when the prices and selection are better.

School teachers have very little time once the school year starts. Thus, applying these rules I'd finish my shopping for holidays and birthdays before the school year started. This was a great time saver and reduced stress once school began.

# Situation 11
## Rules To Live By

Dad thought it horrible if you made choices that put your life in danger or had a high potential to damage your physical being for the remainder of your life.

1. Don't play football as you can get life-long injuries
2. Don't go surfboarding without a partner
3. Don't become a social worker
4. Always hold your keys at night like spiked brass knuckles when walking to your car because your fist with the keys poking out will do more damage if you are attacked. Also, if the person comes up from behind you stomp on the arch of the attacker's foot to throw them off balance prior to attacking with your keys. Then run as if your life depended on it.

Dad also gave us some really fun rules to live by.

1. Explore different religions
2. Treat everyone the same regardless of their job or status.
3. Never tell someone else's joke when they are around. So, remember who told you what jokes and to whom you have told them.

## Make Wise Choices

Dad so valued education that he paid for all five of us to go to college. He made the following points:
- If there is ever a war and/or a natural disaster where everyone loses everything, the people with an education shall eventually recover, yet those without an education will incur hardships for the rest of their lives.
- People with an education are harder to fool and thus will find life easier.
- Educated people realize that there is nothing intelligent about emotions; yet feelings are valuable.

When my dad passed away he left each of us siblings some money. I split this gift from my dad between a portion of the down payment on my house, plus on tuition to further my education. I desired to learn specific skills that had not been covered in public school nor college. Paying for tuition, enhancing my educational base, was the best way ever to utilize my inheritance as it really honored Dad, especially since he stressed education so very much.

# Situation 12
## Eating Habits for Maximum Health

Dad taught us that breakfast was the most important meal of the day. We children were served a well-balanced meal for breakfast, that usually included some type of egg dish for protein and some carbs while Dad had ice cream for his protein and cookies for his carbs explaining the importance of adults eating the most calories in the morning to be able to burn them off during the day. How do you decide what and when to eat?

1. Do you eat to have something to do?
2. Do you eat when not hungry?
3. Do you equate eating with self-love, so you eat to nurture yourself?
4. Do you habitually grab something each time you walk into the kitchen?
5. Do you eat in front of the television set?
6. Do you eat to be social when others are eating?
7. Do you eat "fast food" for its convenience?
8. Do you eat quickly without really tasting your food?

All of these scenarios mean that you are living to eat instead of eating to live per my dad.

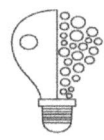

## Dad's Diet to Adjust or Maintain Weight

Dad thought it important to keep eating one's favorite foods so not to feel deprived. This is the diet he suggested to many of his patients to change their eating habits and allow the body to adjust to its perfect weight.

- BREAKFAST: Eat anything and everything you desire, be it lasagna, to ice-cream and cookies.
- LUNCH: one serving of protein and fruit.
- DINNER: one serving of protein and vegetables.
- SNACK: if one does get hungry between meals to eat plain popcorn without salt, butter or other adornments.
- DRINKS: Black coffee, plain tea, and water only.

No alcohol or canola oil allowed when choosing to decrease one's weight as both caused weight gain in his opinion.

## Food Combining Important

This was important to ensure good digestion, even though Dad ignored this for his breakfast.

- Do not eat protein and starches in the same meal.
- Do not eat fruit and veggies in the same meal.

## Situation 13
### Taking Risks Involving Money

You don't get ahead if you don't take risks. The problem is that it's hard to decide if a risk is a valid one or not. So, Dad taught us Connie Dembrowski's* protocol to determine if the risk had merit and then he added to those basics. So, what do you consider before taking a risk? What do you do to minimize the risk factor and maximize the potential benefits?

1. Do you trust the stock broker to give you the best deal while you risk your savings?
2. Do you trust the salesman who is selling an expensive program where the only guarantee is that he makes money?
3. Do you move to a new place where you do not know anyone and don't have a job risking not being able to earn a living?
4. Do you believe in someone's advice when no one else does, so you risk being ostracized from your friends?

*Connie Dembrowski's protocol has three rules:
- The activity is legal.
- You will learn something new.
- It must be a win-win situation when others are involved.

## Question Yourself Prior to Risking Money

- Ask yourself if they are only making money off of selling their program or do they have a bona fide business that makes money as some people are simply marvelous sales people, and nothing else.
- For money markets, you pay each time you are getting in or out of a market, so the one advising you of trading makes the money, not you.
- If you can read a book and teach yourself that way, do it.
- Model others, but don't copy them; if not you are a duplicate of them, not an original and it won't take long before you lose who you really are.
- Only take rich people's suggestions on how to make money for how can you expect someone to show you if they were not able to do it for self?

I watched my dad learn these lessons the hard way when following other's advice, trusting the wrong people, and losing money on stocks, bonds, and investment portfolios. However, my grandfather invested in real estate and utility companies saying there was always money in land and electricity. Grandpa believed in tangibles, not promises on a piece of paper. My mom and her siblings have benefitted greatly from grandpa's investments.

# Situation 14
## Compassion

The dinner table was often the setting for us kids to learn as dad would make comments on different things that had occurred in his office or during his hospital rounds.

1. There was story of the ninety-six year old lady who had never been sick prior to her being admitted to the hospital. My dad asked her what she thought was the reason for her continued good health throughout the years. She attributed her great health to her shot of whiskey each night. So, Dad ordered a shot of whiskey to accompany her dinner each night while she was in the hospital commenting that her shot of whiskey would do far more good emotionally than her not having it.
2. There was the story of the lady who brought her baby, who was dangerously close to death, into Dad's office. Asked why she hadn't brought the baby in sooner, she replied that she didn't have the money and now she was desperate. My dad charged her only $10 and told her she now had a doctor whom she could afford, and to bring her children to him at the first signs of them being sick.

## Compassionate Actions

Compassion for others is not the same as sympathy or any other energy. Compassion is unique unto itself. We ought not to make a decision to do anything without first considering how our actions will affect others.

- Be yourself, do not copy anyone else as our Creator didn't make two snowflakes that were the same and so God did not need two people that were the same.
- Everyone is worth respecting and is worthwhile. Dad advised Ronald Reagan, when Governor of California, on medical issues, and was the physician for many celebrities, and professional athletes. Yet, he treated the orderlies and custodians at the hospital with the same respect he treated the people who had made a name for themselves.
- He constantly reminded us to view things from another's point of view.
- Others were just as important as we were and that we were just as important as everyone else.

Follow the rules:
- *Golden Rule:* Treat others as you wish to be treated.
- *Platinum Rule:* Treat others as they wish to be treated.

## Situation 15
### Know Yourself

You cannot possibly love yourself until you truly know yourself. And, there is no way you can honestly love another if you don't love yourself. Dad stated that we had to know who we were and to accept the parts we liked about self, while constantly striving to improve the parts that were troubling us. Only once we could accept all of us, including the "imperfect" parts, would we be able to accept all of someone else and to love the other person even when they didn't love themselves.

1. Is your self-talk positive or judgmental?
2. Do you reminisce about the good things that happened in the past, or do you obsess on the unpleasant parts?
3. Can you accept a complement without feeling you either need to negate it, or give a complement back?
4. Can you cheer on another even when their win caused you to lose?
5. Can you celebrate another's victory without feeling envious or jealous?
6. Do you consider how your actions will affect the others involved prior to taking action?

## You Are Not a Mistake

Only people make mistakes; not our Creator. Thus, everyone automatically has value because we were created by God.

- Put yourself in the other person's situation to see things from their viewpoint.
- Listen carefully and ask questions if you wish to really know another person.
- Challenge yourself to see the Creator's spark in everyone else so that you realize their importance.
- Put no man ahead of you and put no man behind you. Always consider yourself equal to all others and all others equal to you.
- People were all created to be equal, but that doesn't equate to people all being born in equal circumstances. Thus, it's important to develop compassion not judgment, as we never truly know what another has had to endure.
- Live your life for you, not for others, doing what you feel is important. Let others live their lives by their rules.
- Know which rules to break.

My dad would be thrilled to see that you took your time to let him share some of his life's experiences with you. Will you incorporate some of his understandings into your life?

**You've finished. Before you go…**

Tweet/share that you finished this book.

Please star rate this book.

Reviews are solid gold to writers. Please take a few minutes to give us some itty bitty feedback.

## ABOUT THE AUTHOR

Sharón Lynn Wyeth spent forty years in education, twenty-nine as a teacher, and eleven as an administrator. She did her best to share what she learned from her dad and to treat everyone with kindness and compassion. She summed up her dad's teachings by constantly reminding herself that when a person is the hardest to love, it indicates that they need love the most. So, she challenged herself to do just that.

In the educational field she is well respected, for having created the very first dual high school and college credit classes in the state of Texas; helping to create an incredibly successful dropout prevention program that was highlighted on the Tom Brokaw Evening News and presented at then President Bush Senior's conference for all fifty governors; and for writing an effective one semester program for the Texas Community Colleges on how to bridge the gap between high school and college math that was funded by the Gates Foundation.

Wyeth created other inroads in education, yet her greatest gift to humanity was recognizing the patterns in names which linked to someone's personality and purpose, thus creating Neimology® Science. The most repeated comment from individuals who have had their names read by her is, "You are changing lives!" Indeed, that is what Sharón Lynn Wyeth has been doing her entire life.

If you enjoyed this Itty Bitty® book you might also like…

- **Your Amazing Itty Bitty® Book Keeping Book** – Joe DiChiara

- **Your Amazing Itty Bitty® Dissertation Book** – Dr. Laura Haase and Dr. Anja Thelen

- **Your Amazing Itty Bitty® Gratitude Book** – Belinda Lee Cook

And our many other Itty Bitty books available on line at www.ittybittypublishing.com.

www.ingramcontent.com/pod-product-compliance
Lightning Source LLC
Chambersburg PA
CBHW061305040426
42444CB00010B/2527